Planning for Learning through Space

by Rachel Sparks Linfield. Illustrated by Cathy Hughes

Contents

Making plans 2-3

Using the 'Early Learning Goals' 4-6

EYFS Planning Chart 7

Theme 1: The Earth 8-9

Theme 2: The Sun 10-11

Theme 3: Other stars 12-13

Theme 4: Our moon 14-15

Theme 5: Journeys into space 16-17

Theme 6: Planets, UFOs and the Space Party 18-19

Bringing it all together – Space Party 20

Resources 21

Collecting evidence of children's learning 22

Activity overview 23

Home links 24

Family page Inside back cover

Published by Practical Pre-School Books, A Division of MA Education Ltd,
St Jude's Church, Dulwich Road, Herne Hill, London, SE24 0PB Tel: 020 7738 5454

www.practicalpreschoolbooks.com

Revised (3rd edition) © MA Education Ltd 2013. Reprinted © MA Education Ltd 2012.
First edition © Step Forward Publishing Limited 2008.

Front and back cover images taken by Lucie Carlier © MA Education Ltd.

Planning for Learning through Space ISBN: 978-1-909280-39-7

Making plans

Child-friendly Planning

The purpose of planning is to make sure that all children enjoy a broad and balanced experience of learning. Planning should be flexible, useful and child-friendly. It should reflect opportunities available both indoors and outside. Plans form part of a planning cycle in which practitioners make observations, assess and plan.

Children benefit from reflective planning that takes into account the children's current interests and abilities and also allows them to take the next steps in their learning. Plans should make provision for activity that promotes learning and a desire to imagine, observe, communicate, experiment, investigate and create.

Plans should include a variety of types of activity. Some will be adult-initiated or adult-led, that focus on key skills or concepts. These should be balanced with opportunities for child-initiated activity where the children take a key role in the planning. In addition there is a need to plan for the on-going continuous provision areas such as construction, sand and water, malleable materials, small world, listening area, role-play and mark-making. Thought also needs to be given to the enhanced provision whereby an extra resource or change may enable further exploration, development and learning.

The outdoor environment provides valuable opportunities for children's learning. It is vital that plans value the use of outdoor space.

The UK Frameworks

Within the UK a number of frameworks exist to outline the provision that children should be entitled to receive. Whilst a variety of terms and labels are used to describe the Areas of Learning there are key principles which are common to each document. For example they advocate that practitioners' planning should be personal based on observations and knowledge of the specific children within a setting. They acknowledge that young children learn best when there is scope for child-initiated activity. In addition it is accepted that young children's learning is holistic. Although within the documents Areas of Learning are presented separately to ensure that key areas are not over-looked, within settings, children's learning will combine areas. Thus the Areas of Learning are perhaps of most use for planning, assessment and recording.

Focused area plans

The plans you make for each day will outline areas of continuous provision and focused, adult-led activities. Plans for focused-area activities need to include aspects such as:

- resources needed;
- the way in which you might introduce activities;
- individual needs;
- the organisation of adult help;
- size of the group;
- timing;
- safety;
- key vocabulary.

Identify the learning and the Early Learning Goals that each activity is intended to promote. Make a note of any assessments or observations that you are likely to carry out. After carrying out the activities, make notes on your plans to say what was particularly successful, or any changes you would make another time.

A final note

Planning should be seen as flexible. Not all groups meet every day, and not all children attend every day. Any part of the plan can be used independently, stretched over a longer period or condensed to meet the needs of any group. You will almost certainly adapt the activities as children respond to them in different ways and bring their own ideas, interests and enthusiasms. The important thing is to ensure that the children are provided with a varied and enjoyable curriculum that meets their individual developing needs.

Making plans

Using the book

Read the section which outlines links to the Early Learning Goals (pages 4-6) and explains the rationale for focusing on 'Space'.

The chart on page 7 gives an example format for weekly planning. It provides opportunity to plan for the on-going continuous provision, as well as more focused activities.

Use pages 8 to 19 to select from a wide range of themed, focused activities that recognise the importance of involving children in practical activities and giving them opportunities to follow their own interests. For each 'Space' theme, two activities are described in detail as examples to help you in your planning and preparation. Key vocabulary, questions and learning opportunities are identified. Use the activities as a basis to:

● extend current and emerging interests and capabilities
● engage in sustained conversations
● stimulate new interests and skills

Find out on page 20 how the 'Space' activities can be brought together in a Space Party.

Use page 21 for ideas of resources to collect or prepare. Remember that the books listed are only suggestions. It is likely that you will already have, within your setting, a variety of other books that will be equally useful.

The activity overview chart on page 23 can be used either at the planning stage or after each theme has been completed. It will help you to see at a glance which aspects of children's development are being addressed and alert you to the areas which may need greater input in the future.

As children take part in the activities, their learning will progress. 'Collecting evidence' on page 22 explains how you might monitor each child's achievements

There is additional material to support the working partnership of families and childr

in the form of a reproducible Family Page found inside the back cover.

It is important to appreciate that the ideas presented in this book will only be a part of your planning. Many activities that will be taking place as routine in your group may not be mentioned. For example, it is assumed that sand, dough, water, puzzles, role-play, floor toys, technology and large scale apparatus are part of the ongoing early years experience. Role-play areas, stories, rhymes, singing, and group discussion times are similarly assumed to be happening in each week although they may not be a focus for described activities.

Using the 'Early Learning Goals'

The principles that are common to each of the United Kingdom curriculum frameworks for the early years are described on page 2. It is vital that, when planning for children within a setting, practitioners are familiar with the relevant framework's content and organisation for areas of learning. Regardless however, of whether a child attends a setting in England, Northern Ireland, Scotland or Wales they have a right to provision for all areas of learning. The children should experience activities which encourage them to develop their communication and language; personal, social, emotional, physical, mathematical and creative skills. They should have opportunities within literacy and be encouraged to understand and explore their world.

Within the Statutory Framework for the Early Years Foundation Stage (2012), Communication and Language; Physical Development and Personal, Social and Emotional Development are described as Prime Areas of Learning that are 'particularly crucial for igniting children's curiosity and enthusiasm for learning, and for building their capacity to learn, form relationships and thrive' (page 4, DfE 2012). The Specific Areas of Learning are Literacy, Mathematics, Understanding the World and Expressive Arts and Design.

For each Area of Learning the Early Learning Goals (ELGs) describe what children are expected to be able to do by the time they enter Year 1. These goals, detailed on pages 4 to 6, have been used throughout this book to show how activities relating to 'Space' could link to these expectations. For example, for Personal, Social and Emotional Development one aim relates to the development of children's 'self-confidence and self-awareness'. Activities suggested which provide the opportunity for children to do this have the reference PSE1. This will enable you to see which parts of the Early Learning Goals are covered for a given theme and to plan for areas to be revisited and developed.

In addition, an activity may be carried out to develop a range of different Early Learning Goals. For example, whilst exploring the Sun children can make suns from card and straws. They will develop knowledge of shape and number as they use circles and count rays. In addition, they will explore media and materials and develop aspects of Expressive Arts and Design. Thus, whilst adult-focused activities may have clearly defined goals at the planning stage, it must be remembered that as children take on ideas and initiate their own learning and activities, goals may change.

The Prime Areas of Learning
Communication and Language

Listening and attention: children listen attentively in a range of situations. They listen to stories, accurately anticipating key events and respond to what they hear with relevant comments, questions or actions. They give their attention to what others say and respond appropriately, while engaged in another activity. (CL1)

Understanding: children follow instructions involving several ideas or actions. They answer 'how' and 'why' questions about their experiences and in response to stories or events. (CL2)

Speaking: children express themselves effectively, showing awareness of listeners' needs. They use past, present and future forms accurately when talking about events that have happened or are to happen in the future. They develop their own narratives and explanations by connecting ideas or events. (CL3)

'Space' provides many opportunities for children to enjoy listening, understanding and speaking. When the children discuss the first Moon walk and the importance of the Sun for providing light and heat, or listen to stories about 'Space', they will develop listening, speaking and questioning skills. Games such as travelling to stars chalked on the playground, require the children to follow instructions. The role-play space station encourages children to express themselves and to show awareness of the needs of their peers.

Physical Development

Moving and handling: children show good control and co-ordination in large and small movements. They move confidently in a range of ways, safely negotiating space. They handle equipment and tools effectively, including pencils for writing. (PD1)

Health and self-care: children know the importance for good health of physical exercise, and a healthy diet, and talk about ways to keep healthy and safe. They manage their own basic hygiene and personal needs successfully, including dressing and going to the toilet independently. (PD2)

'Space' offers many opportunities for children to enjoy movement activities and to handle tools and equipment.

When children throw beanbags on to stars, walk on the Moon or travel around the Earth they can develop and demonstrate control and co-ordination. The development of fine-motor skills will come through searching for beads in Moon rocks (play-dough); making planet necklaces and printing stars in clay. Activities relating to Sun safety, and taking exercise on a rocket, will contribute to the development of knowledge of health and self-care. Areas such as basic hygiene and going to the toilet independently, however, will be part of on-going, daily activity and, as a result, PD2 will appear less frequently than PD1 within the described activities for Physical Development.

Personal, Social and Emotional Development

Self-confidence and self-awareness: children are confident to try new activities, and say why they like some activities more than others. They are confident to speak in a familiar group, will talk about their ideas, and will choose the resources they need for their chosen activities. They say when they do or don't need help. (PSE1)

Managing feelings and behaviour: children talk about how they and others show feelings, talk about their own and others' behaviour, and its consequences, and know that some behaviour is unacceptable. They work as part of a group or class, and understand and follow the rules. They adjust their behaviour to different situations, and take changes of routine in their stride. (PSE2)

Making relationships: children play co-operatively, taking turns with others. They take account of one another's ideas about how to organise their activity. They show sensitivity to others' needs and feelings, and form positive relationships with adults and other children. (PSE3)

'Space' offers many opportunities, both for child-initiated and adult-led activities, which will develop children personally, socially and emotionally. When using the role-play space or weather stations; making pictures of stars or considering how to teach aliens manners children have the opportunity to make relationships. When deciding how to decorate Moon boots, or making telescopes from cardboard tubes, children can develop self-confidence and self-awareness. Many of the areas described within the ELGs for Personal, Social and Emotional Development though, will be covered on an almost incidental basis. Any activity that involves collaboration will help children to build relationships whilst self-confidence can be promoted through activities that allow children to show initiative and follow their own trains of thought.

The Specific Areas of Learning
Literacy

Reading: children read and understand simple sentences. They use phonic knowledge to decode regular words and read them aloud accurately. They also read some common irregular words. They demonstrate understanding when talking with others about what they have read. (L1)

Writing: children use their phonic knowledge to write words in ways which match their spoken sounds. They also write some irregular common words. They write simple sentences which can be read by themselves and others. Some words are spelt correctly and others are phonetically plausible. (L2)

Activities for Space based on well-known picture books allow the children to read using both their phonic knowledge and memories of common, irregular words. Discussions of the stories will help children to understand and to develop their vocabularies. Activities, such as addressing envelopes for letters from outer space; writing sentences about the Moon's appearance and words on stars; or making 'Take care of our Earth' posters, will encourage children to explore the sounds within words and to enjoy the early stages of writing.

Mathematics

Numbers: children count reliably with numbers from 1 to 20, place them in order and say which number is one more or

one less than a given number. Using quantities and objects, they add and subtract two single-digit numbers and count on or back to find the answer. They solve problems, including doubling, halving and sharing. (M1)

Shape, space and measures: children use everyday language to talk about size, weight, capacity, position, distance, time and money to compare quantities and objects and to solve problems. They recognise, create and describe patterns. They explore characteristics of everyday objects and shapes and use mathematical language to describe them. (M2)

Activities for Space provide many opportunities for children to count, to measure and to explore shape and space. Observations of planets will encourage children to consider shapes such as circles and spheres. Sorting sequin stars, using the 'Racing Rockets' number rhyme, and making card and straw suns will allow children to count and to compare. Investigation of the size of shadows, over time, stimulates interest in size and measurement. Using the sand tray to simulate a Moon walk, or using toy cars or pedal vehicles to 'drive' around the Earth can be valuable opportunities to encourage the use of positional language.

Understanding the World

People and communities: children talk about past and present events in their own lives and in the lives of family members. They know that other children don't always enjoy the same things, and are sensitive to this. They know about similarities and differences between themselves and others, and among families, communities and traditions. (UW1)

The world: children know about similarities and differences in relation to places, objects, materials and living things. They talk about the features of their own immediate environment and how environments might vary from one another. They make observations of animals and plants and explain why some things occur, and talk about changes. (UW2)

Technology: children recognise that a range of technology is used in places such as homes and schools. They select and use technology for particular purposes. (UW3)

To understand their world children need times to gain knowledge, to explore and to relate what they discover to both previously held ideas and future learning. Clearly activities relating to 'Space' offer valuable opportunities to discover facts about the Earth, the Sun, the Moon and other stars and planets. When exploring constellation patterns, making star shaped biscuits or looking at photos of the local environment and other places on the Earth, children will be able to make comparisons and notice similarities and differences. When taking photos of the local area or using solar powered calculators, children have the opportunity to use and to appreciate technology. Technology will also feature in role-play as well as being part of the on-going, daily

provision. Discussing things that happen in sunny weather will allow children to talk about past and present events in their own lives and in their families' lives.

Expressive Arts and Design

Exploring and using media and materials: children sing songs, make music and dance, and experiment with ways of changing them. They safely use and explore a variety of materials, tools and techniques, experimenting with colour, design, texture, form and function. (EAD1)

Being imaginative: children use what they have learnt about media and materials in original ways, thinking about uses and purposes. They represent their own ideas, thoughts and feelings through design and technology, art, music, dance, role-play and stories. (EAD2)

Whilst involved in activities for Space, children will experience working with a variety of materials, tools and techniques as they paint stars, moons and favourite places on the Earth; decorate sparkly star wands and make models of aliens and UFOs. Doing space dances, and making and playing with space stick puppets, allow the children to be imaginative. Opportunities to explore music come through singing songs such as 'Hey diddle diddle', 'Twinkle, twinkle little star' and 'The Sun has got his hat on'. Throughout all the activities children should be encouraged to talk about what they see and feel as they communicate their ideas in painting, collage, music and role-play.

Note
The Early Learning Goals raise awareness of key aspects within any child's development for each Area of Learning. It is important to remember that these goals are reached through a combination of adult and child-initiated activity within Early Years settings and also a child's home life. Thus, it is vital that goals are shared by practitioners and parents, and children are given every opportunity to develop throughout their Early Years Foundation Stage at home and within a setting.

Week beginning:	Monday	Tuesday	Wednesday	Thursday	Friday
FOCUSED ACTIVITIES					
Focus Activity 1:					
Focus Activity 2:					
Stories and rhymes					
CONTINUOUS PROVISION (Indoor)					
Collage					
Construction (large)					
Construction (small)					
ICT					
Imaginative play					
Listening					
Malleable materials					
Mark making					
Painting					
Role play					
Sand (damp)					
Sand (dry)					
Water					
CONTINUOUS PROVISION (Outdoor)					
Construction					
Creative play					
Exploratory play					
Gross motor					
ENHANCED PROVISION (Indoor)					
ENHANCED PROVISION (Outdoor)					

Theme 1: The Earth

Communication and Language

- Discuss ways to take care of the Earth such as not dropping litter, turning off taps, recycling and switching off lights. (CL2)
- Look at a globe. Show the children that the Earth is a sphere. Find places on the globe that the children have visited. What were the places like? Would the children like to revisit the places? (CL3)

Physical Development

- Talk about how the earth spins. Enjoy playing with spinning hoops and balls. (PD1)
- Talk about the Earth traveling through space. Enjoy blowing bubbles outside. Which 'Earth' travels the furthest? (PD1)
- Outside use chalk to draw a large Earth. Enjoy using the Earth for movement activities. Encourage children to 'paddle' in the sea, 'drive' to Wales and 'fly' to France. (PD1)

Personal, Social and Emotional Development

- Enjoy co-operative play in a role-play weather station. Encourage children to use globes and maps, to give forecasts and to suggest new resources to include in their weather station. (PSE3)
- Look at photos of rubbish dumps. Talk about recycling. Help the children to understand the need to use materials sensibly and to know how they can help to take care of the Earth. (PSE2)

Literacy

- Begin a display of questions about the Earth and Space. Help the children to ask and write questions and over the weeks to find answers in non-fiction books. (L2)
- Make posters to encourage people to take care of the earth. (L2)
- Address envelopes to be sent to the Earth from space (see activity opposite). (L2)
- Enjoy reading stories that include a range of settings such as *Elmer* by David McKee (jungle) *Percy the Park Keeper* by Nick Butterworth (forest) and *Harry and the Dinosaurs* by Ian Whybrow (town and country). (L1)

Mathematics

- Sort a box of 3-D shapes to find 'spheres like the Earth'. (M2)
- Use three different sized circles of coloured paper to make a picture of the inside of the Earth (see activity opposite). (M2)
- Use toy cars and road layouts to 'drive' around the Earth. Reinforce language for positions and directions. (M2)

Understanding the World

- Talk about how the Earth turns to create day and night. Draw pictures of animals and people that are awake during the night. (UW2)
- Use travel brochures to make a display of pictures that show features on the Earth such as mountains, hills, seas and deserts. (UW2)
- Look at pictures to show the Earth in space. Explain that it is one planet in the Solar System. (UW2)
- Enjoy taking photographs of the local environment. Compare the pictures with ones in books of places on the Earth. How are they similar or different? (UW2, 3)

Expressive Arts and Design

- On circles of white paper use green and blue smudged pastels or chalks to make pictures of the earth as seen from space. (Note: When finished, an adult in a well ventilated area can 'fix' the Earths with hairspray.) (EAD1)
- Talk about the different climates and weathers around the world. Paint pictures to show favourite places visited by the children or ones they would like to go to. (EAD2)

Activity: Letters from space

Learning opportunity: Writing on envelopes.

Early learning goal: Literacy. Writing.

Resources: Picture of the Solar System, envelopes, pencils, a used envelope with an address on it.

Key vocabulary: Solar System, Earth, address, envelope.

Organisation: Small group.

What to do: Show the children an envelope with an address on it. Point out the different features such as the street, the village/town, the county and the postal code.

Next, look at the picture of the Solar System. Identify the Earth.

Ask the children to imagine they were on another planet, way out in Space and wanted to send a letter to someone on the Earth. Together write an address, but this time, go further to include the country, the Earth and the Solar System. Provide envelopes for the children to enjoy writing their own addresses and sticky labels to use as stamps.

Activity: Making circle collages of the Earth

Learning opportunity: Using size and shape vocabulary.

Early learning goal: Mathematics. Shape, space and measures.

Resources: Colourful paper circles in three different sizes (e.g.12cm, 18cm and 20cm diameters; glue.)

Key vocabulary: Earth, circle, biggest, smallest, core, mantle, crust.

Organisation: Small group.

What to do: Cut a fruit such as an orange, a plum or a nectarine in half.

Explain that it is a bit like the Earth in that it has a centre, a middle part and an outer layer. Show the children a picture of the inside of the Earth and point out the core, mantle and crust.

Provide a basket of paper circles in different colours and sizes. Tell the children that they can be used to make pictures of the Earth. Encourage the children to use the word 'circle' and size vocabulary and to say how many circles they will each need. Make colourful pictures to show the Earth's cross section.

Display

Make a 'Take care of our Earth' board to display the climate paintings and posters. On a table put out two boxes labelled 'waste paper' and 'plastic' to encourage the children to recycle. Cover a second board with black sugar paper and a blue border. Put up the pastel Earths interspersed with the circles that show the structure of the Earth. Make a post box from a large cardboard box, painted red. Put up the envelopes as if falling from the box.

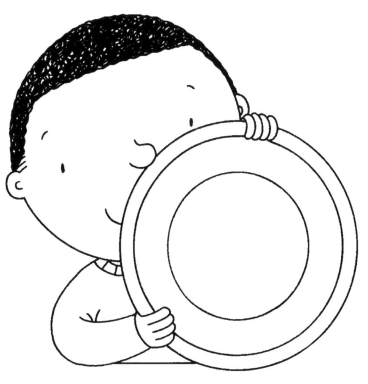

Theme 2: The Sun

Communication and Language

- Explain that the Sun is a star, a giant ball of very hot gas. Talk about the importance of the Sun for providing heat and light. (CL1)
- Make a collection of storybooks that include illustrations of the Sun. Share the stories and discuss what happens and why. (CL1, 2)

Physical Development

- Play the hot/cold game (see activity opposite). (PD1)
- In pairs, move as a person and their shadow. Encourage the children to move slowly so that the shadow and person make identical movements together. (PD1)
- Talk about sun safety. Look through picture books to find characters that are sensibly wearing sunhats and clothing with sleeves. (PD2)

Personal, Social and Emotional Development

- Make plans for a picnic to take place on a sunny day. Encourage children to consider the clothes they will need such as sunhats and T-shirts with sleeves. (PSE1, 3)

Literacy

- Write sun acrostics with single words or phrases. (L2) (e.g. **S**hining brightly
  Umbrellas protect us
  Never cold)
- Make a collection of words that rhyme with 'sun' and with 'hot'. How many words can be read before the sand runs through a timer? (L1, 2)
- Make 'Sun Safety' posters. (L2)

Mathematics

- Compare the sizes of shadows at different times of the day. (M2)
- Make repeating patterns from paper suns in a variety of sizes. (M2)
- Make shadow paintings using 2D plastic shapes (see activity opposite). (M2)
- Make suns from circles of orange card and rays made from pieces of orange or yellow straws. Which sun has the most rays? Does any sun have 10 rays? (M1)

Understanding the World

- Grow cress in the light and the dark to demonstrate the importance of the Sun for plants. (UW2)
- Investigate how to make shadows by blocking light. What shapes can hands make? What do they look like? (UW2)
- Talk about solar power. Enjoy playing with solar-powered calculators. (UW3)
- Talk about events that take place in sunny, warm weather. Did the children enjoy them? (UW1)

Expressive Arts and Design

- Make collages of the Sun. Cover the reverse side of small paper plates with overlapping pieces of orange, red and yellow papers. Varnish the Suns with watered down PVA glue. (EAD1)
- Paint pictures to show people enjoying sunny days. (EAD2)
- Enjoy singing 'The Sun has got his hat on' (traditional). Make up actions for the words. (EAD1)

Activity: Shadow shapes

Learning opportunity: Recognising and using shapes.

Early learning goal: Mathematics. Shape, space and measures.

Resources: 2-D shapes cut from stiff card, paint in three different colours, black paper, stiff, thick paint brushes.

Key vocabulary: Names for the 2-D shapes and paint colours, shadow.

Organisation: Small group.

What to do: Remind the children of how shadows are formed. Look at the 2-D shapes and encourage the children to name them. Demonstrate how shape shadows can be made by laying a shape on the black paper, pressing on it with a finger and using a stiff paint brush to stipple (press) paint along the edge of the shape. When dry, enjoy matching the shapes with their own shadows.

Activity: The hot/cold game

Learning opportunity: Listening to instructions and moving with control.

Early learning goal: Physical Development. Moving and handling.

Resources: A paper sun.

Key vocabulary: Hot, cold, sun, hide, find, words to describe movements.

Organisation: Small group.

What to do: Prepare for the activity by hiding the sun. Tell the group that you have hidden a paper sun in the room. Ask the group to look for the sun. As they search provide clues such as "Leanne you are very cold." "Stanley you are extremely hot!" Repeat the activity encouraging the children to move in different ways. Also, invite children to hide the sun and to give clues. If playing the game outside use a small orange or yellow ball as the sun.

Display

Cover a board with sky blue paper and make a sunny display using the paper plate suns and the acrostics. On small cloud-shaped pieces of paper write words that describe the Sun to intersperse with the other display items. Laminate some of the shape shadow paintings and place these on a table with shapes to lie on the shadows.

Theme 3: Other stars

Communication and Language

- Share storybooks that include a star. (CL1)
- Make up a group story about a new star (see activity opposite). (CL3)
- Outside draw on the playground a variety of stars. Give instructions for ways to travel between the stars and actions to perform on a star. (CL2)

Physical Development

- Provide a variety of objects to use for making star prints in rolled out pieces of clay. (PD1)
- Use playground chalk to draw a number of stars outside. Enjoy aiming beanbags into the stars. (PD1)

Personal, Social and Emotional Development

- Show the group pictures of stars. Invite children to select materials and collaborate to make pictures of stars on A4 sized pieces of black paper. (PSE3)
- Sometimes we say someone is a 'star'. Talk about the things people could do to 'be a star' (PSE2)

Literacy

- On stars, cut from card, write regular words. Encourage children to use their phonic knowledge to decode the words. (L1)
- Invite children to select two 'star words' and use them to write a sentence about Space. (L2)

Mathematics

- Make collages of stars from shiny triangles, circles and squares. Encourage the children to name the shapes as they choose to use them. (M2)
- Give each child a concertina book made from blue paper with pages labeled from 1 to 9. Ask children to stick or draw the matching number of stars. (M1)
- Sort sequin stars by size and/or colour. Count how many are in each group. (M1)

Understanding the World

- Make constellation patterns (see activity opposite). (UW2)
- Use non-fiction books and the internet to find out information about stars. (UW3)
- Make star shaped biscuits. Encourage children to describe the ingredients and to compare the uncooked dough with the cooked biscuits. (UW2)

Expressive Arts and Design

- Sing 'Twinkle, twinkle little star'. Encourage the children to do actions and to use tuned and un-tuned percussion instruments to make 'starry music'. (EAD1)
- Make wands from plastic straws and shiny card stars. Encourage the children to enjoy using them in magical role-play. (EAD2)
- Use runny paint and black paper to make blow paintings of shooting stars. (EAD1)

Activity: Making a group star story

Learning opportunity: Collaborating to make up a story.

Early learning goal: Communication and Language. Speaking.

Resources: Any picture book about a star, star cut from shiny card.

Key vocabulary: Star

Organisation: Whole group, sitting on the floor, in a circle.

What to do: Share a story about a star. As you read encourage the children to notice descriptive words and facts about the star. Explain that as a group you are going to make up a story about a new star.

Remind the group about 'listening eyes' that look at the person who is speaking.

Hold the card star and begin to tell the story. Describe a child, going to bed, drawing the curtains and suddenly noticing a large, bright star.

Ask for a volunteer to continue the story and give them the star. Explain that whoever has the star can tell the story. After a few lines, ask the child to pass the star on around the circle.

Children can then choose whether to speak or whether to listen and pass the star on.

Activity: Making constellations

Learning opportunity: Making star shapes/patterns.

Early learning goal: Understanding the World. The world.

Resources: Sticky, shiny stars; A4 sized black paper, pictures of star constellations including the Plough.

Key vocabulary: Plough, star, numbers to 10, constellation.

Organisation: Small group.

What to do: Show the children a picture of the Plough constellation. What do the children think it looks like? Explain that on a clear night the stars can be seen in the sky to make up the Plough pattern. Look at other star constellations. How many stars make up the shapes? What does the shape look like?

Tell the children that they can make up their own constellation with up to ten stars. Talk about shapes they might like to try. As a group do a boat, house or hat shape. Give out the paper and stars for the children to do their own constellations. Encourage the children to give their constellations names.

Display

Put up the shiny star collages and constellations as a giant patchwork in a corner of a room that can be used for role-play. From the ceiling hang streamers of black and dark blue crepe paper to create a feeling of night. Put out cushions, toy animals that would be out at night, a box of books depicting stars and a bucket containing the wands. Encourage the children to visit the night corner to enjoy magical role-play.

Theme 4: Our Moon

Communication and Language

- Talk about what it must have felt like to be the first man to walk in space. Enjoy role-playing the first space walk. (CL1)
- Give instructions for making televisions from cereal packets turned inside out. Paint pictures of the first Moon walk to display on the 'television screens'. (CL2)

Physical Development

- Enjoy pretending to take Moon walks. (PD1)
- Remind the children that the Moon is a sphere and enjoy playing with large balls. (PD1)
- Give children lumps of black or grey playdough containing hidden beads. How many beads can they find in the 'Moon rocks' before a minute has passed? (PD1)

Personal, Social and Emotional Development

- Astronomers use telescopes to observe the Moon. Invite children to collaborate to make model telescopes, choosing their own resources. Use the telescopes for role-play. (PSE1, 3)

Literacy

- Make a group book entitled 'The Moon looks like...' (L1, 2)
- Write new versions of the nursery rhyme 'Hey, diddle, diddle, the cat and the fiddle' (see activity opposite). (L1, 2)
- Talk about people who help us by working at night. Make thank you cards for the people. (L2)

Mathematics

- Use the sand tray for Moon role-play to practise using positional language (see activity opposite). (M2)
- Cut out full, half and new Moons from card. Use them for sorting and counting activities. (M1)

Understanding the World

- Make a record of the phases of the Moon. Ask the children to look out for the Moon each night or morning and to record its shape. (UW2)
- Explain we see the Moon because it reflects sun light. Place objects in a black box with small peep-holes. Provide torches to be sunlight shining on the objects. (UW2)
- Use books and the internet to find pictures of animals that could be seen on a moon-lit night. Use finger paints and black paper to make pictures of owls. (UW2, 3)

Expressive Arts and Design

- Look at pictures to show the phases of the Moon. On strips of black paper use white paint to show some of the Moon shapes. (EAD1)
- Paint pictures to illustrate the new verses for 'Hey diddle, diddle' (see Literacy). (EAD2)

Activity: Hey, diddle, diddle, names

Learning opportunity: Reading and writing.

Early learning goal: Literacy. Reading. Writing.

Resources: Words from 'Hey diddle, diddle' written on separate postcards, paper, pens, pencils and postcards.

Key vocabulary: Words within 'Hey diddle, diddle'.

Organisation: Small group.

What to do: Recite the nursery rhyme 'Hey diddle, diddle, The cat and the fiddle, The cow jumped over the Moon ...' Show the children the word cards and ask them to find the word 'cow' and also 'jumped'. Tell the children that it would be good to have some new verses for the rhyme. Ask for suggestions of other animals and also for what they might do (e.g. 'The lion leapt over the Moon!'). Encourage children to write the ideas in postcards, and to read their new verses.

Activity: Moon walks

Learning opportunity: Using positional language in role-play.

Early learning goal: Mathematics. Shape, space and measures.

Resources: Set out the sand tray as the Moon with craters, mountains, a car (moon buggy), play figures (astronauts) and rocket (made from cardboard tube covered with foil).

Key vocabulary: Positional language, crater, rocket, astronaut.

Organisation: Small group.

What to do: Invite a small group to visit the Moon. Show them the craters and mountains. Ask a child to land the rocket on top of a mountain. Ask a second child to drive the Moon buggy in front of the rocket. Encourage the children to play and to use positional language as they move the rocket, astronauts and space buggy. Finish the playing with a countdown to take the rocket back to the Earth.

Display

Cut out the night animals and display them on a board covered with black paper with a full moon, trees and shiny stars. Invite children to say where they would like their animals to be placed. On a second board put up the 'Hey, diddle, diddle' pictures. In a box place the lines they illustrate. Each day select a line and ask the children to match it to its picture. Use the black strips of moons as a border for the displays.

Theme 5: Journey into space

Communication and Language

- Enjoy sharing picture books that include space travel and rockets. (CL1)
- Set out a table as a role-play space station with walkie talkies, star charts, paper, pencils and safe binoculars/ a telescope. Encourage children to be people who talk to astronauts on missions in space. (CL3)

Physical Development

- Use large equipment to pretend to be astronauts climbing into a rocket. (PD1)
- Role-play travelling in rockets. (PD1)
- Use pencils to decorate paper rockets with dots, lines and swirls. (PD1)

Personal, Social and Emotional Development

- When astronauts travel through space they have to get used to living close together in a small area. Talk about how it would feel to be an astronaut and rules that might be useful for living in a rocket. (PSE2)
- Look at a picture of an astronaut's clothes. Explain what each part does. Give each child a 'space boot' cut from paper. Encourage children to decide how they would like to decorate the space boots and to select their own materials. (PSE1)

Literacy

- Write a count down poem where each line gives an in instruction to the astronauts (e.g. '10 Climb in the rocket'). (L2)
- Talk about the special food that astronauts eat in space. On rocket shaped paper make menus for astronauts. (L2)

Mathematics

- Enjoy doing count downs from a variety of numbers. (M1)
- Sort solid shapes into cones and cylinders. Make rockets from cardboard tubes, and cones made from cardboard circles cut to the centre. (M2)
- Use the 'Racing Rockets' rhyme (see activity opposite). (M1)

Understanding the World

- Use the internet to find pictures of things astronauts might see in space. (UW3)
- Talk about the use of parachutes, in some space missions, for taking parts of the rocket back to Earth. Make parachutes from 20-30cm squares of tissue paper or plastic carrier bag with taped on thread attached to a small weight. Investigate which parachute falls the slowest. (UW2)

Expressive Arts and Design

- Make 'gloopy' space paintings on black paper (see activity opposite). (EAD1)
- Use card and lolly sticks or plastic straws to make stick puppets of rockets and astronauts. Use them to imagine travelling to space. (EAD2)
- Make paper planes as space shuttles. Decorate them with crayon (pen ink makes the paper curl) and enjoy launching the shuttles in a large space. (EAD1)
- Describe the first walk on the Moon. Explain that the astronauts placed a flag on the Moon to celebrate. Provide materials from which children can select items to make flags. Use the flags in role-play. (EAD2)

Activity: Racing Rockets number rhyme

Learning opportunity: Recognising numerals and counting.

Early learning goal: Mathematics. Numbers.

Resources: Postcard sized rockets cut from card and numbered 1 to 9.

Key vocabulary: Rocket, race, missing, numbers 1 to 9.

Organisation: Whole group.

What to do: Show the children the rockets. As a group place them in number order, count them and then pick them up.

Recite the rhyme and on 'go', drop seven of the rockets. Together place the rockets that have landed in order and ask the children to say which ones are missing.

9 rockets have a race
Flying down to Earth from space.
Ready, steady, get set, go! (Drop some of the rockets on 'go'.)
Are any missing do you know?

Repeat the rhyme with different numbers of landing rockets and encourage the children to give actions to the words.

Activity: Gloopy space paintings

Learning opportunity: Pattern making with fingers.

Early learning goal: Expressive Arts and Design. Exploring and using media and materials.

Resources: Large sheets of black sugar paper; table coverings, overalls, pictures of space, gloopy paint in three different colours made from 4 cups of flour, 1 cup of sugar, ready mixed paint and approximately 2 cups water dependent on required consistency. (Note: For small quantities, use an egg cup as the measure.)

Key vocabulary: Words to describe the colours, gloopy paint and patterns.

Organisation: 2 children.

What to do: Show the children the space pictures. Talk about the colours, the stars, the planets and rockets.

Show the children the gloopy paint. Ensure that sleeves are rolled up and clothes are covered. Let the children feel the paint and describe the texture. Invite them to paint a space picture with their hands.

Display

Combine the gloopy paintings to make a space background at child height. If possible hang the cardboard tube rockets from the ceiling in front of the background, or place them at varying heights on the display. On a nearby table put the stick puppets and invite children to explore space!

Theme 6: Planets, UFOs and the Space Party

Communication and Language
- Talk about the forthcoming space party. Make plans for games to play and food to eat. (CL3)
- Enjoy sharing stories that feature aliens (CL1)

Physical Development
- Talk about the variety in sizes of the planets and features such as Jupiter's moons and Saturn's rings. Enjoy playing with moons and planets (balls of different sizes) and rings (hoops). (PD1)
- Thread spherical beads to make planet necklaces. (PD1)
- Astronauts have medicals to pass before they are allowed to travel in space. In the rockets they do special exercises to use their muscles to keep fit. Discuss how children can keep healthy on Earth. Role-play taking exercise in a rocket. (PD1, 2)

Personal, Social and Emotional Development
- Provide old T-shirts, to decorate with fabric pens/crayons, for dressing up as UFOs, aliens and astronauts at the space party. (PSE1)
- Tell the children that if an alien visited they would need to teach it a lot of things such as manners, how to behave and how to show its feelings. Role-play helping an alien. (PSE2)

Literacy
- Explain that UFO stands for 'Unidentified Flying Object'. Use children's initials to make up descriptive phrases e.g. EHL – Edmund Hates Liquorice; RESL – Rosie Eats Sloppy Leeks. Write the phrases on strips of card. Encourage children to enjoy reading their own phrases. (L2)
- Sing and make up new lines for the 'Alien Song' (see activity opposite). (L1, 2)

Mathematics
- Use a picture of the Solar System to practise counting and to compare sizes. (M1, 2)
- Make a collage of a UFO or an alien, using regular 2-D shapes. Encourage the children to use shape vocabulary as they play 'I spy an alien/UFO that has ...' with shape clues. (M2)

Understanding the World
- Look at pictures of the planets. Talk about their characteristics. (UW2)
- Having first checked with carers for food allergies, decorate circular, plain biscuits as planets for the Space Party. Compare the biscuits with pictures of the real planets to find similarities and differences. (UW2)
- Use the internet to find interesting facts about the planets. Print out children's favourite ones. (UW3)

Expressive Arts and Design
- Use excerpts from *The Planets Suite* by Holst to make space dances. (EAD2)
- Provide boxes, pipe cleaners, paper scraps, tape etc to make aliens and UFOs. (EAD2)
- Use milk, food dye and washing up liquid to watch 'space patterns' (see activity opposite). (EAD1)

Activity: Singing the Alien Song

Learning opportunity: Making actions for a song.

Early learning goal: Literacy. Reading. Writing.

Resources: Flipchart, pen.

Key vocabulary: Alien, snout, ten.

Organisation: Whole group.

What to do: Tell the children that there are many things still to discover in space. Explain that so far, the Earth is the only known planet that has living things on it. What might be alive on an unknown planet? Sing the alien song, to the tune of 'I'm a little teapot' (Traditional), with actions.

I'm a little alien short and stout,
I've ten fingers and one snout.
When I see the rocket hear me shout
Take me in to fly me out.

On a flipchart sketch a short creature to fit the one in the song. Ask for ideas for other features such as antennae, a tail etc. and sketch these. Write new lines such as: 'I'm a little alien with one toe, I've antennae and I glow.' (N.B. Lines do not have to rhyme.) Encourage children to write new lines, to read the new verses and enjoy singing the song.

Activity: Food dye space patterns

Learning opportunity: Describing and recording patterns.

Early learning goal: Expressive Arts and Design. Exploring and using media and materials.

Resources: For each group white paper circles, crayons/felt pens, shallow dish of milk, washing up liquid, food colouring, dropper/straw. (NB The dish must be clean.)

Key vocabulary: Words to describe colours and movement, space, UFO.

Organisation: Small group.

What to do: Remind the children that a UFO is something in space that no one can identify. Tell the children to imagine that the dish of milk is space and that in a moment they will see UFOs. Drop a few drops of food dye on to the surface of milk in a shallow dish. In the centre place a drop of washing up liquid and ask the children to describe what they see (Note: the dye should quickly disperse giving a moving pattern.) Provide circles of paper for the children to draw the patterns that they see.

On further occasions, make up space dances and move like the food dye.

Display

Place boxes on a large table or on the floor in a safe corner. Cover them with a black, navy or blue piece of cloth – a sheet is ideal. Arrange the alien models and the white circles with patterns, to make a space display. Nearby, place a box of percussion instruments and the words for the alien song for the children to use during times of independent choosing.

Bringing it all together

The Space Party makes an enjoyable end to the activities related to 'Space'. Children have the opportunity to wear costumes, play space themed games and enjoy special refreshments.

Preparation

Ask parents to donate large, unwanted, plain T-shirts for children to decorate with fabric crayons/pens, sticky shapes etc as astronauts, aliens or UFOs. Provide tin foil, cardboard tubes, card strips, sticky dots, straws, pipe cleaners and small boxes for props such as walkie-talkies and antennae.

Decorate the room where the party will take place with strips of black crepe paper on which the children have stuck shiny card shapes as planets, rockets and stars. Use balloons, to hang up as extra planets.

Decorate circular biscuits as planets, gingerbread men as astronauts and bake half moon, shortbread biscuits. Cut chunks of carrot as the Sun and thick slices of cucumber as UFOs. Mix a variety of fruit juices to make a colourful, space drink to have with straws.

The party

Start the Space Party with a count down followed by an imaginary journey into space. Tell a story which encourages the children to mime travelling in space. Finish with them arriving on Planet X. Say that it is an unknown planet and to celebrate its discovery you are going to play some games. Space themed games could include:

- Pass the stars (based on pass the parcel) – Children sit in a circle. A child shakes a die and a plastic container of sticky stars is passed on the corresponding number of places. The child who receives the container takes out a star and the die is shaken again.
- Musical planets – Music is played for the children to dance. When the music stops the children stand in one of a number of hoops or chalked circles which are named after the planets. All the children standing in a given planet gain a star.
- Pin the nose on the alien.
- Keep the planet in space – pairs of children have a balloon. Everyone does a countdown and on 'blast off' the children tap their balloon and compete to see which pair can keep their balloon in the air the longest.

Having already checked with carers what their children may eat, enjoy sharing the space refreshments. Conclude the event by inviting the parents and carers to join the group to sing space songs learnt during the topic. For the final song, to the tune of 'John Brown's Body' (Traditional), sing one verse and chorus of:

We're on a rocket to take us back to Earth (x3)
Take us back to Earth.
Zooming past the stars and planets (x3)
Take us back to Earth!

Land with a spoken count down from 10 and finish with 'SPLASH DOWN!'

Resources

Resources to collect:

- Unwanted, clean, plain, large T-shirts
- Fabric pens/crayons (an iron may be required to fix the colour)
- Child-friendly binoculars/telescope
- Plastic mirrors
- Globe
- Spherical beads and thread
- Long cardboard tubes
- Junk mail envelopes
- Cress seeds
- Hoops and balls
- Balloons

Everyday resources

- Large and small boxes including cereal packets and shoe boxes
- Papers and cards of different weights, colours and textures e.g. sugar, tissue, silver and shiny papers corrugated card, etc.
- Paint, different sized paint brushes and a variety of paint mixing containers
- A variety of drawing and colouring pencils, crayons, pastels, felt pens etc.
- Glue and scissors
- Additional decorative and finishing materials such as sequins, foils, glitter, tinsel, shiny wool and threads, beads, pieces of textiles, parcel ribbon
- Table covers
- Lolly sticks, match sticks and off-cuts of wood
- Malleable materials such as play-dough
- Playground chalk
- Masking tape

Stories

All of the following books were available from leading booksellers at the time of writing. None of them are specifically needed for the described activities but they represent a selection of well-known stories available about space. When planning for the topic, however, look through the books already within your setting. It is likely that you will find good alternatives. For non-fiction resources consider using the internet for pictures.

- *Q Pootle 5 In Space* by Nick Butterworth
- *Laura's Star* by Klaus Baumgart
- *By the Light of the Moon* by Sheridan Cain and Gaby Hansen
- *Aliens Love Underpants* by Claire Freedman and Ben Cort
- *Wanda and the Alien* by Sue Hendra
- *Small Billy and the Midnight Star* by Nette Hilton and Bruce Whatley
- *Meg on the Moon* by Helen Nicholl and Jan Pienkowski
- *Owl Babies* by Martin Waddell
- *The Owl Who Was Afraid of the Dark* by Jill Tomlinson
- *Zoom Rocket Zoom* by Margaret Mayo
- *Alien Tea on Planet Zum-Zee* by Tony Mitton

Songs

- *Okki-tokki-unga: Action Songs for Children* by Beatrice Harrop

Resources for planning

- **England:** Statutory framework for the Early Years Foundation Stage (2012) (www.foundationyears.org.uk/early-years-foundation-stage-2012)
- **Northern Ireland:** CCEA (2011) 'Curricular Guidance for Pre-school Education' (www.rewardinglearning.org.uk/curriculum/pre_school/index.asp) CCEA (2006) Understanding the Foundation Stage (www.nicurriculum.org.uk/docs/foundation_stage/UF_web.pdf)
- **Scotland:** Learning and Teaching Scotland (2010) 'Pre-birth to Three: Positive Outcomes for Scotland's Children and Families' (www.ltscotland.org.uk/earlyyears/). The Scottish Government (2008) 'Curriculum for Excellence: Building the Curriculum 3 – A Framework for Learning and Teaching' (www.ltscotland.org.uk/buildingyourcurriculum/policycontext/btc/btc3.asp)
- **Wales:** Welsh Assembly (2008) 'Framework for Children's Learning for 3 to 7-year-olds in Wales' (http://wales.gov.uk/topics/educationand skills/schoolshome/curriculuminwales/arevised curriculumforwales/foundationphase/?lang=en)

Collecting evidence of children's learning

Monitoring children's development is an important task. Making a profile of children's achievements, strengths, capabilities interests and learning will help you to see progress and will draw attention to those who are having difficulties for some reason. If a child needs additional professional help, such as speech therapy, these cumulative profiles will provide valuable evidence.

Profiles should cover all the areas of learning, as defined by the relevant UK framework, and be the result of collaboration between practitioners, parents and carers. Parents should be made aware of your record keeping policies when their child joins your group. Show parents the types of documentation that you are keeping and make sure they understand their purpose. As a general rule, documentation should be open. Families should have access to their child's documentation at any time and know they can contribute to it. Take regular opportunities to talk to parents about children's progress. If you have formal discussions regarding children about whom you have particular concerns, a dated record of the main points should be kept.

Keeping it manageable

Documentation should be helpful in informing practitioners, adult helpers and parents and always be for the benefit of the child. The golden rule is to keep it simple, manageable and useful. Do not try to make records following every activity!

Documentation will basically fall into two categories – observations and reflections:

Observations

- **Spontaneous observations:** Sometimes you will want to make a note of observations as they happen e.g. a child is heard counting cars accurately during a play activity, or is seen to play collaboratively for the first time.

- **Planned observations:** Sometimes you will plan to make observations of children's developing skills within a planned activity. Using the learning opportunity identified for an activity will help you to make appropriate judgments about children's capabilities, strengths and interests, and to record them systematically.

To collect information:

- Talk to children about their activities and listen to their responses.
- Listen to children talking to each other.
- Observe children's work such as early writing, drawings, paintings and models. (Keeping photocopies or photographs can be useful in tracking progress. Photographs are particularly useful to monitor children's development in the outdoor environment.)

Sometimes it may be appropriate to set up 'one off' activities for the purposes of monitoring development. Some groups at the beginning of each term, for example, ask children to write their name and to make a drawing of themselves to record their progressing skills in both co-ordination and observation.

Reflections

It is useful to spend regular time reflecting on the children's progress. Aim to make some comments about each child each week, and discuss these regularly with colleagues and families.

Informing your planning

Collecting evidence about children's progress is time consuming and it is important that it is useful. When planning, use the information collected to help you to decide what learning opportunities you need to provide next for each child. For example, a child who has poor pencil or brush control will benefit from more play with dough or construction toys to build strength of muscles in the hands and fingers.

Example observation sheet

Name: Lucy Field

Date: 17.1.13

Area of Learning: Mathematics. Count reliably with numbers from 1 to 20.

Context (Please tick):

Child-initiated: √   **Adult-led:**
Alone: **In a group:** √

Observation: Lucy is playing outside with two friends. She is trying to build the tallest tower and counting the bricks. "1, 2, 3, 4, 5, 7, 8. Mine's 8. Yours is only 7." She knocks the tower down, chuckles and starts to build again, counting as she places the bricks. "1, 2, 3, 4, 5, 7." The tower falls over. "Oh blow. I wanted to do 20."

What next: Check Lucy knows 6 follows 5. Encourage use of the outdoor counting grids, skittles and number rhyme CD.

Observer: E. M. Hogg

Overview of areas covered through 'Space'

	Communication and Language	Physical Development	Personal, Social and Emotional Development	Literacy	Mathematics	Understanding the World	Expressive Arts and Design
The Earth	Listening and attention Understanding Speaking	Moving and handling Health and self-care	Self-confidence and self-awareness Managing feelings and behaviour Making relationships	Reading Writing	Numbers Shape, space and measures	People and communities The world Technology	Exploring and using media and materials Being imaginative
The Sun	Listening and attention Understanding Speaking	Moving and handling Health and self-care	Self-confidence and self-awareness Managing feelings and behaviour Making relationships	Reading Writing	Numbers Shape, space and measures	People and communities The world Technology	Exploring and using media and materials Being imaginative
Other stars	Listening and attention Understanding Speaking	Moving and handling Health and self-care	Self-confidence and self-awareness Managing feelings and behaviour Making relationships	Reading Writing	Numbers Shape, space and measures	People and communities The world Technology	Exploring and using media and materials Being imaginative
Our moon	Listening and attention Understanding Speaking	Moving and handling Health and self-care	Self-confidence and self-awareness Managing feelings and behaviour Making relationships	Reading Writing	Numbers Shape, space and measures	People and communities The world Technology	Exploring and using media and materials Being imaginative
Journey into space	Listening and attention Understanding Speaking	Moving and handling Health and self-care	Self-confidence and self-awareness Managing feelings and behaviour Making relationships	Reading Writing	Numbers Shape, space and measures	People and communities The world Technology	Exploring and using media and materials Being imaginative
Planets, UFOs and the Space Party	Listening and attention Understanding Speaking	Moving and handling Health and self-care	Self-confidence and self-awareness Managing feelings and behaviour Making relationships	Reading Writing	Numbers Shape, space and measures	People and communities The world Technology	Exploring and using media and materials Being imaginative

Note: For each theme, highlight the Early Learning Goal areas covered through both adult focused and child-initiated activities relating to 'Space'.

Home links

The theme of space lends itself to useful links with children's homes and families. Through working together children and adults gain respect for each other and build comfortable and confident relationships.

Establishing partnerships

- Keep parents informed about the activities for 'Space' and the themes for each week. By understanding the work of the group, parents will enjoy the involvement of contributing ideas, time and resources.
- Photocopy the Family page for each child to take home.
- Invite friends, child minders and families to share in the singing at the end of the Space Party.

Visiting enthusiasts

- Invite adults known to the group, who work at night, to talk about what the Earth is like when most people are asleep.
- If a parent has an interest in astronomy, invite them to come in to answer questions asked by the children.

Resource requests

- Catalogues, greetings cards, colour supplement magazines, wallpaper, wrapping paper, fabric, wool, and shiny materials are invaluable for collage work and a wide range of interesting activities.
- Ask parents to donate unwanted:
  Large plain T-shirts;
  Picture books about Space – fiction and non-fiction;
  Clean envelopes e.g. from junk mail.

The Space Party

It is always useful to have extra adults for parties. Involve them in helping to prepare and set out the refreshments, put up decorations, blow up balloons and in dressing their children for the party.